D1032714

DISCARD

Dedicated
to
Louis Ginsberg,
Poet

T.V. Baby Poems

T.V. Baby Poems

Allen Ginsberg

GROSSMAN PUBLISHERS INC. IN ASSOCIATION
WITH CAPE GOLIARD, LONDON
NEW YORK   1968

✓ 811
Ginsberg,
A

Copyright © 1968 Allen Ginsberg
Library of Congress No. 68-15647

TELEVISION WAS A BABY CRAWLING
TOWARD THAT DEATH CHAMBER

It is here, the long Awaited bleap-blast light that Speaks one red tongue like
    Politician, but happy its own govt.,
either we blow ourselves up now and die, like the old tribe of man, arguing
    among neutrons, spit on India, fuck Tibet, stick up America,
    clobber Moscow, die Baltic, have your tuberculosis in Arabia, wink
    not in Enkidu's reverie—
it's all a long Train of Associations stopped for gas in the desert & looking
    for drink of old-time H_2O—
made up of molecules, it ends being as innocent as Lafcadio afraid to get up
    & cook his bacon—
I prophesy : the Pigs won't mind ! I prophesy : Death will be the old folks
    home !
I prophesy : Chango will speak on the National Broadcasting System,
I prophesy, we will all prophesy to each other & I give thee happy tidings
    Robert Lowell and Jeanette MacDonald,
Sudden moonlight, starbeam riding its own flute, soul revealed in the
    scribble, an ounce of looks, an Invisible Seeing, Hope ; The
    Vanisher betokening Eternity
one finger raised warning above his gold eyeglasses—and Mozart playing
    giddy-note an hour on the Marxist gramophone—
All Be—let the Kaballah star be formed of perfect circles in a room of 1950
    unhappiness where Myrna Loy gets lost—
The Bardo Thodol extends in the millions of black jello for every dying
    Mechanic—We will make Colossal movies—
We will be a great Tantric Mogul & starify a new Hollywood with our
    unimaginable Flop—Great Paranoia !
The Family presents, your Corpse Hour—attended by myriads flies—with
    hyperactive Commentators freed at their most bestial—sneering,
    critical, literary—perhaps a captive & lone Square
caught hiding behind a dummy-univac in the obscurest Morgues of stran-
    gest Hearst—wherever—no more possible—
Only remains, a photo of a riverswollen hand in black and white, arm
    covered by agèd burlap to the wrist—
skin peeling from the empty fingers— ; Yet discovered by a mad Negro
    high on tea & solitary enough himself to notice a Fate—
therefore, with camera remembered and passed along by hand and mail and
    roaring Jet toward Chicago, Big Table empty this morning,
nothing but an old frog-looking editor worried about his Aesthetics,
That's Life—retired to New York to invent Morse Code & found a great
    yellow telegraph—

Merry Xmas Paul Carrol and Irving Rose in Thrall—give up thy song & flower to any passing Millenium!

I am the One, you are the One, we are the One, A. Hitler's One as well as fast as his Many heavenly Jews are reborn,

many a being with a nose—and many with none but an ear somewhere next to a Yelling Star—

I myself saw the sunflower-monkeys of the Moon—but they spent their dear play-money electricity in a homemade tape-record minute of cartoony high Sound—

There Farewell, as repeated by Wagner, toward the Immortal in many a gladdened expanding mid-europe Hour,

That I'll be hearing forever if the world I go to's Music, Yes good to be stuck on that aching Liebestod Note thru Eternity

which has been playing out there always for me, and for all, whoever can hear enough to write down for a day to let men fiddle in space, blow temporary brass tuba or wave stick at a physical orchestra

and remember the Wagner-music in his own titty-head Consciousness—ah yes that's the Message—

That's what I came here to compose, that's what I knocked off my life to Inscribe on my grey metal typewriter,

borrowed from somebody's lover's mother who got it from Welfare, all interconnected and gracious a bunch of Murderers

as possible in this Kalpa of Hungry blood-drunkard Ghosts—We all have to eat—us Beings

that must gnaw bones and suck marrow and drink living white milk from heavenly Breasts or from bucktoothed negress or wolf-cow.

The sperm bodies wriggle in pools of vagina, in the Yin, that reality we must have spasmd our Beings upon—

The brothers and sisters die if we live, the Myriads Invisible squeak reptile complaint

on Memory's tail which us pterodactyl-buzzard-dove-descended two foot mammal-born Geek-souls almost Forget—

Grab—a cock—any eye—bright hair—All Memory & All Eternity now, reborn as One—

no loss to those—the Peacock spreads its cosmic-eye Magnificat-feathered tail over its forgotten Ass—

The being roars its own name in the Radio, the Bomb goes off its twenty years ago,

I hear Thy music O my mystery, my Father in myself, my Mother in my eye, Brother in my hand, Sister-in-honey on my own Poetry's

Tongue, my Hallelujah Way beyond all mortal inherited Heavens,
O my own blind ancient Love-in-mind !
Who? but us all, a Me, a One, a Dying Being, The Presence, now, this desk,
this hand running over the steps of imagination
over the ladder of letters on the machine, vibrating in humm-herald Extend-
hope of own unto my Thee, returning infinite-myriad at the Heart,
that is only red blood,
that is where murder is still innocence, that life ate,—The white plasmic
monsters forage in their fleet Macrocosm—bit apple or black huge
bacteria gods loomed out of nowhere, potent
maybe once victorious on Saturn in dinasaur-inspired messy old hallucinated
war—
same battle raging in starved cats and haggard dogs of American ghostly
bone—man and man, fairy against red, black on white on white, with
teeth going to the dentist to escape in gas—
The President laughs in his chair, and swivels his head on his neck controlling fangs of Number—
bacteria come numberless, atoms count themselves a greatness in their
pointy own Empire—
The Neutrons of Russia spy on all Conspiracy—& Chinese & yellow energy
waves have ocean and Empyrean ready against attack & future
starvation—Korean principalities of photon are doubles in all but
name—differing Princes of the Art of Electron divide as many as
the tribes of the Congo—Africa's a vast jail of Shadows—
My molecules are numbered, mirrored in all Me robot radiant parts, &
navel marked,—teeth & gullet ingest the living dove-life, foreimage
of the Self-Maw Death Is Now ;
—but there is the Saintly Meat of the Heart—and my feeling to thee O
Peter and all my Lords—these Decades of American loves and car-
rides and vowsworn faces lain on my breast, —my head on many
more naked than my own sad hoping flesh—
our feelings ! come back to the heart—to the old blind hoping Creator home
in his own Mercy, beating everywhere behind machine-hand-
clothes-man-Senator iron powerd or fishqueen-fugitive-com'd
lapel—

Here I am—Old Betty Boop whoopsing behind the skull-microphone
wondering what Idiot soap horror-show we broadcast by Mistake—
full of communists and frankenstein cops and
mature capitalists running the State Department and the Daily News
Editorial hypnotizing millions of legional-eyed detectives to commit
mass murder on the Invisible

which is only a bunch of women weeping hidden behind the newspapers in
    the Andes, conspired against by Standard Oil,
which is a big fat fairy monopolizing all Being that has form'd it self to Oil,
and nothing gets in its way so it grabs different oils in all poor mystic
    aboriginal Principalities too weak to
Screech out over the radio that Standard Oil is a bunch of spying Business-
    men intent on building one Standard Oil in the whole universe like
    an egotistical cancer
and yell on Television to England to watch out for United Fruits they got
    Central America by the balls
nobody but them can talk San Salvador, they run big Guatamala puppet
    armies, gas Dictators, they're the Crown of Thorns
upon the Consciousness of poor Christ-indian Central America, and the
    Pharisees are US Congress & Publicans is the American People
who have driven righteous bearded faithful pink new Castro 1961 is he mad?
    who knows—Hope for him, he stay true
& his wormy 45-year dying peasants read Death's beauty sugar beyond
    politics, build iron children schools
for alphabet molecule stars, that mystic history & giggling revolution
    henceforth no toothless martyrs be memorized by some pubescent
    Juan who'll smoke my marihuana—
Turn the Teacher on!—Yes not conspire dollars under navytown board-
    walk, not spy vast Services of gunny Secrecy under drear eyeglass
    Dulles to ASSASSINATE!
INVADE! STARVE OUT! SUPPLY INVISIBLE ARMS! GIVE
    MONEY TO ORGANIZE DEATH FOR CUBAN REV-
    OLUTION! BLOCKADE WHAT FRAIL MACHINERY!
MAKE EVIL PROPAGANDA OVER THE WORLD! ISOLATE
    THE FAITHFUL'S SOUL! TAKE ALL RICHES BACK!
    BE WORLDLY PRINCE AND POWER OVER THE UN-
    BELIEVABLE! MY GOD!
MAN WORKING IN ELECTRICITY BE U.S. SADISTS THEIR
    MAGIC PHANOPOEIAC THRU MASS MEDIA THE
    NASTIEST IN THIS FIRST HISTORY!
EVIL SPELLS THRU THE DAILY NEWS! HORRIBLE MASO-
    CHISMS THUNK UP BY THE AMERICAN MEDICAL
    ASSOCIATION! TAXES ON YOUR HATE FOR THIS
    HERE WAR!
LEGIONS OF DECENCY BLACKMAIL THY CINEMAL FATE!
    CONSPIRACIES CONTROL ALL WHITE MAGICIANS!
    I CAN'T TELL YOU MY SECRET STORY ON TV!

Chambers of Commerce misquote Bob Hope who is a grim sex revolutionist
      talking in hysterical code
Jimmy Durante's kept from screaming to death in the movies by a huge
      fat Cardinal, the Spell Man, Black Magician he won't let mad
      white Chaplin talk thru the State Megaphone! He takes evil pix
      with Swiss financial cunt!
It's the American Medical Association poisoning the poets with their
      double-syndicate of heroin cut with money-dust,
Military psychiatrists wear deathly uniforms it's Tanganyikan nerve-skin
      in the submarinic navy they're prepared for eternal solitude, once
      they go down they turn to Reptiles
human Dragons trained to fly the air with bomb-claws clutched to breast
      & wires entering their brains thru muffled ears—connected to what
      control tower—jacked to what secret Lab where the macrocosm-
      machine
picks up vibrations of my thought in this poem—the attendant is afraid—
      Is the President listening?
Evil Eye, the invisible police-cop-secrecy masters Controlling Central
      Intelligence—do they know I took Methedrine, heroin, mushrooms
      & lambchops & guess toward a Prophesy tonight?
No the big dopes all they do is control each other—Doom!
in the vast car America—they're screeching on two mind-wheels on a Nat-
      ional Curve—the Car that's made to die by Mr.
Inhuman Moneyhand, by advertising nastyhead Inc. Dream Cancer Prexy
      Owner Distributor Publisher & T V Doctor of Emotional Break-
      down—he told that Mayor to get in that car without his pubic hair
      and drive to Kill get to Las Vegas so the oldfashioned Jewish
      communists
wouldn't get their idealistic radio program on the air in time to make
      everybody cry in the desert for the Indian Serpent to come
back from the Oklahoma mound where he hid with his 15,000,000 visionary
      original Redskin patriot wives and warriors—they made up one big
      mystic serpent with its tail-a-mouth like a lost Tibet
MURDERED AND DRIVEN FROM THE EARTH BY US
      JEWISH GOYIM who spend fifty billion things a year—things
      things!—to make the things-machinery that's turned the worlds of
      human consciousness into a thing of War
wherever and whoever is plugged in by real filaments or wireless or
      whatever magic wordy-synapse to the money-center of the mind
whose Eye is hidden somewhere behind All mass media—what makes

reporters fear their secret dreamy news—behind the Presidential
mike & all its starry bunting, front for some mad BILLIONAIRES
who own United Fruits & Standard Oil and Hearst The Press and
Texas NBC and someone owns the Radios some other owns vast
spheres of Air—

State Legislatures filled with Capital Punishment Fiends because nobody's
been in love on US soil long enough to realize We who pay the
Public Hangman make State Murder thru Alien Gas who cause
any form of hate-doom hanging

do that in public everybody agreed by the neck suffering utmost pangs each
citizen himself unloved suicides him, because there's no beloved,
now in America for Each and All in the gas chamber the whole
California Legislature

screaming because its Death here—we're so hopeless—The Soul of America
almost died with ugly Chessman—strange saintly average madman
driven to think for his own killers, in his pants and shirt and with
human haircut, said NO to—like a Cosmic NO—from the One
Mouth of America speaking Life or Death—looked in the eye by
America—

Ah what a cold monster OneEye he must've saw thru the Star Spangled
Banner & Hollywood with ugly smile forbidden movie & old
heartless Ike in the White House officially allowing Chatterly
attacked by Fed Lawyers—

vast Customs agencies searching books—who Advises what book where—
who invented what's dirty? —tender Genet burned by middleaged
vice Officers

sent out by the Automatic Sourface that mongers whatever bad news he can
high up from imaginary Empire name Scripps-Howard News Of
The World—just more drear opinions—Damn that World
Telegram was Glad Henry Miller's depression Cancerbook not
read to sad eyeglass Joe messenger to Grocer

in Manhatten, or candystore emperor Hersh Silverman in Bayonne, dream-
ing of telling the *Truth*, but his Karma is selling jellybeans & being
kind,

The Customs police denyd him his Burroughs they defecated on De Sade,
they jack'd off, and tortured his copy of Sodom with Nitric Acid in
a backroom furnace house at Treasury Bureau, pouring Fire on the
soul of Rochester,

Warlocks, Black magicians burning and cursing the Love-Books, Jack be
damned, casting spells from the shores of America on the inland
cities, lacklove-curses on Eyes which read genital poetry—
O deserts of deprivation for some high school'd gang, lone Cleveland that
delayed its books of Awe, Chicago struggling to read its magazines,
police and papers yapping over grimy gossip skyscraped from some
sulphurous yellow cloud drift in from archtank hot factories make
nebulous explosives near Detroit—smudge got on Corso's Rosy
Page—
US Postmaster, first class sexfiend his disguise told everyone to open letters
stop the photographic fucks & verbal suckeries & lickings of the
asshole by tongues meant but for poison glue on envelopes Report
this privileged communication to Yours Truly We the National
Police—We serve you once a day—you humanical Meat creep-
hood—
and yearly the National Furnace burned much book, 2,000,000 pieces mail,
one decade unread propaganda from Vietnam & Chinese mag
harangues, Engelian
dialectics handmade in Gobi for proud export to top hat & tails Old Bones
in his penthouse on a skyscraper in Manhatten, laconic on two
phones that rang thru the nets of money over earth, as he barked
his orders to Formosa for more spies, abhorred all Cuba sugar from
concourse with Stately stomachs—
That's when I begin vomiting my paranoia when Old National Skullface
the invisible sixheaded billionaire began brainwashing my stomach
with strange feelers in the Journal American—the penis of billionaires depositing professional semen in my ear, Fulton Lewis *coming*
with strychnine jizzum in his voice making an evil suggestion that
entered my mouth
while I was sitting there gaping in wild dubiety & astound on my peaceful
couch, he said to all the taxidrivers and schoolteachers in brokendown
old Blakean America
that Julius and Ethyl Rosenberg smelled bad, he sent to kill them with
personal electricity, his power station is the spirit of generation
leaving him thru his asshole by Error, that very electric entered
Ethyl's eye
and his tongue is the prick of a devil he don't even know, a magic capitalist
ghosting it on the lam after the Everett Massacre—fucks a
Newscaster in the mouth every time he gets on the Microphone—

and those ghost jizzums started my stomach trouble with capital punishment
—Ike chose to make an Artificial Death for them poor spies—if
they were spying on me? who cares?— Ike disturbed the balance of
the cosmos by his stroke-head deathshake, "NO"
It was a big electrocution in every paper and mass media, Television was a
baby crawling toward that deathchamber
Later quiz shows prepared the way for egghead omlette, I was rotten, I was
the egghead that spoiled the last supper, they made me vomit more
—whole programs of halfeaten comedians sliming out my Newark
relatives assholes—
They used to wash them in the 30's with Young Politics Ideas, I was too
young to smell anything but my own secret mind, I didn't even
know assholes basic to Modern Democracy—What can we teach
our negroes now?
That they are Negroes, that I am thy Jew & thou my white Goy & him
Chinese? —They think they're Arab Microcosms now!
My uncle thinks his Truthcloud's Jewish—thinks his name is Nose-smell-
Newark-5-decades— & that's all except there's Gentile Images of
mirrory vast Universe—
and Chinese Macrocosms too, a race of Spade macrocosms apart, like Jewish
Truth Clouds & Goyisha Nameless Vasts
But I am the Intolerant One Gasberg from the Morgue & Void, Garbler
of all Conceptions that myope my eye & is Uncle Sam asleep in the
Funeral Home—?
Bad magic, scram, hide in J. E. Hoover's bathingsuit. Make his pants fall
in the ocean, near Miami—
Gangster Crash! America will be forgotten, the identity files of the FBI
slipt into the void-crack, the fingerprints unwhorled—no track
where He came from—
Man left no address, not even hair, just disappeared & Forgot his big
wallstreet on Earth—Uncle I hate the FBI it's all a big dreamy
skyscraper somewhere over the Mutual Network—I dont even
know who they are—like Nameless—

Halooo I am coming end of my Presidency—Everybody's fired—I am a
hopeless whitehaired congressman—I lost my last election—
landslide for Readers Digest—not even humans—
Nobody home in town—just offices with many jangling telephones &
automatic switchboards keep the message—typewriters return yr

calls oft, Yakkata yak & tinbellring—THE POLICE ARE AT
THE DOOR—
What are you doing eccentric in this solitary office? a mad vagrant Creep
Truthcloud sans identity card—It's Paterson allright—anyway the
people disappeared—Downtown Fabian Bldg. branch office for
The Chamber of Commerce runs the streetlights
all thru dark winter by univac piped from Washington Lobby—they've
abolished the streets from the universe—just keep control of
the lights—in case of ectoplasm trafficking thru dead Market— where the
Chinese restaurant usta play Muzak in the early century—soft
green rugs & pastel walls—perfumed tea—   `
Goodby, said the metal Announcer in doors of The Chamber of Commerce
—we're merging with NAM forever—and the NAM has no door
but's sealed copper 10 foot vault under the Federal Reserve Bldg.—
Six billionaires that control America are playing Scrabble with antique Tarot
—they've just unearthed another Pyramid—in the bombproof
Cellar at Fort Knox
Not even the FBI knows who—They give orders to J. E. Hoover thru the
metal phonegirl at the Robot Transmitter on top of RCA—you
can see new Fortune Officers look like spies from 20 floors below with their
eyeglasses & gold skulls— silver teeth flashing up the shit-mouthed
grin —weeping in their martinis ! There is no secret to the success
of the
Six Billionaires that own all Time since the Gnostic Revolt in Aegypto—
they built the Sphinx to confuse my sex life,
why are they starting that war all over again in Laos over Neutral Mind?
Is the United States CIA army Legions overthrowing somebody
like Angelica Balibanoff?
Six thousand movietheaters, 100,000,000 television sets, a billion radios,
wires and wireless criscrossing hemispheres, semaphore lights
and morse, all telephones ringing at once to connect every mind
by its ears to one vast consciousness at This Time's Apocalypse—
everybody waiting for one mind to break thru—
Man-prophet with two eyes Dare all creation with his dying tongue & say
I AM—Messiah swallow back his death into his stomach, gaze thru
great pupils of his Bodies' eyes
and look in each Eye man, the eyeglassed fearful byriad-look that might be
Godeyes see thru Death—that now are clark & ego reading manlaw
—write newsbroadcasts to cover with Fears their

own Messiah that must come when all of us conscious—Breakthru to all
          other Consciousness to say the Word I Am, I Am as spoken by a
          certain God —Millenia knew and waited till this one Century—
Now all sentience broods and listens—contemplative & hair full of rain for
          15 years inside New York—what millions know and hark to hear—
many strange magicians in buildings listening inside their own heads—or
          clouds over Manhattan Bridge—or strained thru music messages
          come &
blow the Cosmic Horn to waken every Tiglon & Clown sentience through-
          out the vasting circus—in the Name of God to pick up the tele-
          phone and call the Networks announcing Suchness that
I Am mutter a million old Gods in their beards, that had been sleeping at
          evening radios—Talking to myself again
said the Messiah turning a dial to remember his last broadcast—Calling All
          Beings—in dirt from the ant to the most frightened Prophet that
          ever clomb tower—that all lone
soul in Iowa or Hark-land join the Lone, set forth, walk naked like a
          Hebrew king, enter the human cities and speak free, at last the
          Man-God come that
hears all Phantasy behind the matter-babble in his ear, and walks out of his
          Dream into the cosmic street
open mouth to the First Consciousness—God's woke up now, you Seraphim,
          call Men with trumpet microphone & telegraph, hail every sleep-
          walker with Holy Name,

Life is waving, the cosmos is sending a message to itself, its image is
          reproduced endlessy over TV
over the radio the babble of Hitler's and Claudette Colbert's voices got
          mixed up in the bathroom radiator
Hello hello are you the Telephone the Operator's singing we are the
          daughters of the universe
get everybody on the line at once plug in all ears by laudspeaker, newspeak,
          secret message,
handwritten or electronic impulse travelling along rays the electric spiderweb
Magnetisms shuddering on one note We We We, mustached disc jockeys
          trembling in mantric exitement, flowers bursting in patterns over
          the couch,
drapes falling to the floor in St.-Jean Perse's penthouse, Portugal's water is
          running in all the faucets on the SS Santa Rosa,

chopping machines descend on the pre-dawn tabloid, the wire services are
       hysterical and send too much message,
they're waiting to bam out the Armageddon, millions of rats reported in
       China, smoke billows out New York Hospital's furnace smokestack,
I am writing millions of letters a year, I correspond with hopeful messengers
       in Detroit, I am taking drugs
and leap at my postman for more correspondence, Man is leaving the earth
       in a rocket ship,
there is a mutation of the race, we are no longer human beings, we are one
       being, we are Being connected to itself,
it makes me crosseyed to think how, mass media assemble themselves like
       congolese Ants for a purpose
in the massive clay mound an undiscovered huge Queen is born, Africa
       wakes to redeem the old Cosmos,
I am masturbating in my bed, I have dreamed of a new Stranger who
       touched my heart with his eye,
he hides in a loft on sidestreet in Hoboken, the heavens have covered East
       Second Street with Snow,
all day I walk in the wilderness over white carpets of City, we are redeeming
       ourSelf, I am Born, I seize power over the Universe—
Yawk, Mercy the Octopus, it's It cometh over the Void & makes whistle
       its lonemouthed flute You-Me Forever—
Stop Arguing, Cosmos, I give up so I be, I receive a happy letter from
       Ray Bremser exiled in New Jersey jail—

Dawn of the ages! Man thy Alarm rings thru sweet myriad mornings in
       every desperate-carred street! Saints wait in each metropolis for
       Message to Assassinate the old idea, that 20000 yr old eye-god
Man thought was Being Secret in its Mystery, Unbearable Judge above,
       The One Unknown, alien God handless & tongueless to poor man,
       who'll scream for mercy on his Deathbed—Oh I saw that black
Octopus as Death, with spikes of supernatural antennae raying the Awful
       in waves at my consciousness, a huge dark Ball invisible, behind all
       rooms in the universe—A not-a-man—a no-one—Mystery—
       Nobodaddy
Omnipotent Telepath more visionary than my own Prophetics & Memories
       —Reptile-sentient shimmer-feel-hole in the cosmic Here,
Dense Soullessness wiser than Time, the Eater-Darkness hungry for All—
       but must wait till I leave my own body to enter that

One Mind nebula to my recollection—Unendurable, but my soul dared
    not die,
Shrank from that monster radiating crockodilian Implacabilities from the
    door-mind in its breast, touch Him and the hand's destroyed,
Death God of the End, dwelling in His Eternity, before the Timeworld of
    creation—
I mean some kind of monster from another dimension is eating Beings of
    our own Cosmos—
I saw him and he tried to make me leave my corpse-illusion of an Allen,
    myth movie world come to the celluloid-end,
I screamed seeing myself in reels of death my consciousness a cinematic toy
    played once in a faded attick by man-already-forgotten
His orphan starhood inked from Space, the movie industry itself blot up
    with History & all wracked myriad Epics, Space wiped itself out,
lost in a crack of the wall of a dream it had once disappearing—maybe
    trailing endless cometlong trackless thru what unwonted dimensions
    it keeps dreaming into existence that it can die inside of—as they
    vanish like this Cosmos of Stars I am turning to bones in—
That much illusion, and what's visions but visions, and these words filled
    Methedrine —I have a backache & 2 telegrams come midnight
    from messengers that cry to plug in the Electrode Ear to
my skull downstreet, & hear what they got say, big lives like trees of
    Cancer in Bronx & Long Island—Telephones connect the void
    islands blissy darkness scattered in many minds——

One Winter Day   New York City   1961

PORTLAND COLOSEUM

A brown piano in white
        round spotlight,
Leviathan auditorium
        ribbed and wired,
     hanging organs, vox
       black battery—
A single whistling sound of
        ten thousands childrens'
      larynxes asinging
pierce the ears, and
       flowing up the belly
       bliss the moment arrived

Apparition, four brown
        jacket christhair boys
Goofed Ringo batting bright
       white drum,
Silent George hair patient
      Soul horse,
Short black-skulled
       Paul with thin guitar
Lennon the Captain, his mouth
        a triangular smile,
all jump together to end
    some tearful memory song
     ancient two years,

    the million children
    the thousand worlds
bounce in their seats, bash
       each other's sides, press
       legs together nervous
        as black knees move
         the musicians,
Scream again & claphand
      become one Animal
       New World Auditorium
—hands waving myriad
      snakes of thought
       screetch beyond hearing

while a line of police with
       folded arms stands
Sentry to contain the red
       sweatered ecstasy
      that rises upward to the
        wired roof.

8/27/65

FIRST PARTY AT KEN KESEY'S WITH HELL'S ANGELS

Cool black night thru redwoods
cars parked outside in shade
behind the gate, stars dim above
the ravine, a fire burning by the side
porch and a few tired souls hunched over
in black leather jackets. In the huge
wooden house, a yellow chandelier
at 3AM the blast of loudspeakers
hi-fi Rolling Stones Ray Charles Beatles
Jumping Joe Jackson and twenty youths
dancing to the vibration thru the floor,
a little weed in the bathroom, girls in scarlet
tights, one muscular smooth skinned man
sweating dancing for hours, beer cans
bent littering the yard, a hanged man
sculpture dangling from a high creek branch,
children sleeping softly in bedroom bunks,
And 4 police cars parked outside the painted
gate, red lights revolving in the leaves.

DEC 1965

MIDDLE OF A LONG POEM ON 'THESE STATES'

Kansas City to St Louis

Leaving K.C. Mo.   past Independence   past Liberty
Charlie Plymell's memories of K.C. renewed
       The Jewel-box Review,
           white-wigged fat camps yakking abt
           Georgie Washington and Harry T.
       filthier than any poetry reading I ever gave
              applauded
      by police negro wives   Mafia subsidised
To East St. Louis on the broad road
   Highway 70 crammed with trucks
  Last night almost broke my heart dancing to
          Cant Get No Satisfaction
lotsa beer & slept naked in the guest room—
                       Now
Sunlit wooded hills overhanging the highway
rolling toward the Sex Factories of Indiana—
      Automobile graveyard, red cars dumped
      bleeding under empty skies
     Birchfield's paintings, Walker Evans' photos,
     White Victorian house on a hill—
Trumble & bung of chamber music
        pianoesque on radio—midwest Culture
          before rock and roll
If I knew twenty years ago   what I know now
I coulda led a symphony orchestra in Minneapolis
       & worn a tuxedo—

Heart to heart, the Kansas voice of Ella Mae
     "Are you afraid of growing old,
   afraid you'll no longer be attractive to your husband?
  . . . I don't see any reason" says the radio
                "for those Agitators—
  Why don't they move in with the negroes? We've been separated all
along, why change things now? But I'll hang up, some other Martian might
want to call in, who has another thought."—The Voice of Leavenworth
       echoing thru space to the car dashboard
    ". . . causes and agitations, them, then they're doing the work
of the communists as J. Edgar Hoover says, and many of these people are
people with uh respectable, ability, of a cloak of respectability that shows uh
uh teachers professors and students . . ."
       hollow voice, a minister
       breathing thru the telephone

"God created all the races . . . and it is only men who tried to mix em up, and when they mix em up that's when the trouble starts."

"No place like Booneville though, buddy—"
          End of the Great Plains,
                    late afternoon sun, rusty leaves on trees
               One of these days those boots will walk all over you
We The People   shelling the Vietcong
     "Inflation has swept in upon us . . . Johnson administration rather than a prudent Budget . . . discipline the American people rather than discipline itself . . ."

I lay in bed naked in the guest room,
          my mouth found his cock,
                    my hand under his behind
                         Till the whole body stiffened
                              and sperm choked my throat.
Michel, John Lennon & Paul McCartney
     wooing the decade
          gaps from the '30s returned—
                                   Old earth
rolling mile after mile patient
     The ground
               I roll on
                    the ground
                    the music soars above
The ground electric arguments
                                   ray over
The ground dotted with signs for Dave's Eat Eat
     scarred by highways, eaten by voices
                    Pete's Cafe—
                         Golden land in the setting sun
Missouri River icy brown, black cows,
     grass tufts standing up hairy on hills
               Spring one month to come.
Sea shells on the ground strata'd by the turnpike—
     Old ocean evaporated away,
               Mastadons stomped, dinasaurs groaned
               when these brown hillocks were
          leafy steam-green-swamp-think
                              Marsh nations

before the Birch Society was a gleam in the Pterodactyl's eye
—Aeroplane sinking groundward
    toward my white Volkswagon, prehistoric
      white cockroach under high tension wires—
            My face, Rasputin in car mirror.

Funky barn, black hills approaching Fulton
    where Churchill rang down the Curtain
                on Consciousness
and set a chill which overspread the world
    one icy day in Missouri
                not far from the Ozarks—
Provincial ears heard Spenglerian Iron
                Terror Pronouncement
        Magnificent Language, they said,
            for county ears—
St Louis calling St Louis calling
    Twenty years ago,
            Thirty years ago
                the Burroughs School
Pink cheeked Kenney with fine blond hair,
    his almond eyes aristocrat
                gazed,
        Morphy teaching English & Rimbaud
                at midnight to the fauns
        W.S.B. leather cheeked, sardonic
            waiting for change of consciousness,
                unnamed in those days—
        Coffee, vodka, night for needles,
            young bodies
                beautiful unknown to themselves
            running around St Louis
    on a Friday evening
        getting drunk in awe & honor of the
                terrific future these
red dry trees at sunset go thru two decades later:
            They could've seen
the animal branches, wrinkled to the sky
        & known the gnarled prophecy to come,
if they'd opened their eyes outa the whiskey-haze
                in Mississippi riverfront bars

and gone into the country w/ a knapsack to smell the ground.
    Oh grandfather maple and elm!
Antique leafy old oak of Kingdom City in the purple light
    come down, year after year,
        to the tune
          of mellow pianos.
Salute, silent wise ones,
    Cranking powers of the ground,
   awkward arms of knowledge
    reaching blind above the gas station
      by the high TV antennae
Stay silent, ugly Teachers,
  let me & the Radio yell about Vietnam and mustard gas.

      "Torture . . . tear gas legitimate weapons . . .
Worries language beyond my comprehension" says the radio
     commentator himself.
Use the language today
    ". . . a great blunder"
     in Vietnam, heavy voices,
"A great blunder . . . once you're in, uh,
  one of these things, uh . . ."
"Stay in." Withdraw,
    Language, language, uh, uh
   from the mouths of Senators, uh
     trying to think on their feet
       Saying uhh, politely
Shift linguals, said Burroughs, *Cut the Word Lines!*
   He was right all along.
        ". . . a procurer of these dogs . . .
take them from the United States . . . Major Caty . . . as long as it's
not a white dog . . . Sentry Dog Procurement Centre, Texas . . . No dogs,
once trained, are ever returned to the owner . . ."
              French Truth

Dutch Civility
     Black asphalt, blue stars,
      tail light procession speeding East,
The hero surviving his own murder,
   his own suicide, his own
     addiction, surviving his own
  poetry, surviving his own
     disappearance from the scene—

returned in new faces, shining
        through the tears of new eyes.
            New small adolescent hands
                        on tiny breasts,
            pale silken skin at the thighs,
                and the cherry-prick raises hard
                    innocent heat pointed up
                    from the muscular belly
of basketball highschool English class spiritual Victory,
            made clean at midnight in the bathtub of old City,
                        hair combed for love——
millionaire body from Clayton or spade queen from E St Louis
            laughing together in the TWA lounge——
Past blue-lit airfields into St Louis,
        past billboards' ruddy neon,
            looking for the old hero renewed
                    in a new decade——
        Kleig lights scanning th'evening horizon
Body by Fischer,
            painted by Morris,
                Miller Hi-Life in his hand?
Hill-wink of houses,
        thin bones of aluminium sentinelled dark
        on the suburban hump bearing high wires
                    for thought to traverse
            river & wood, from hero to hero——
        Monotone road grey-bridging the streets
        emblemed with Flouresan & Normandy——
Crane all's well, the wanderer returns
                    from the west with his Powers,
        the Shaman with his beard
                    in full strength,
        the longhaired Crank with subtle humorous voice
                        enters city after city
            to kiss the eyes of your high school sailors
            and make laughing Blessing
                    for a new Age in America
spaced with concrete but Souled by yourself
                        with Desire,
or like yourself of perfect Heart, adorable
            and adoring its own millioned population
                    one by one self-wakened

under the radiant signs
     of Power stations stacked above the river
highway spanning highway,
                bridged from suburb to suburb.

March 1966

Yellow Budweiser signs over oaken bars,
"Ive seen everything"—the bartender giving me change of $10,
I stared at him amiably eyes thru an obvious Adamic beard—
with Montana musicians homeless in New York, teen age
curly hair themselves—we sat at the antique booth & gossiped,
Madame Grady's literary salon a curious value in New York—
"If I had my way I'd cut off your hair and send you to Vietnam"—
"Bless you then" I replied to a hatted thin citizen hurrying to the
      barroom door
upon wet dark Amsterdam Avenue decades later—
"And if I couldn't do that I'd cut your throat" he snarled farewell,
and "Bless you sir" I added as he went to his fate in the rain, dapper
      Irishman.

April 1966

CITY MIDNIGHT JUNK STRAINS
FOR FRANK O'HARA

Switch on lights yellow as the sun
              in the bedroom . . .
The gaudy poet dead   Frank O'Hara's bones
          under grass
An emptiness at 8 PM in the Cedar Bar
      Throngs of drunken
        guys talking about paint
    & lofts, and Pennsylvania youth.
        Klein attacked by his heart
& chattering Frank
     stopped forever—
   Faithful drunken adorers, mourn.
        The busfare's a nickel more
    past his old apartment 9th Street by the park.
Delicate Peter loved his praise,
    I wait for the things he says
              about me—
    Did he think me an Angel
      as angel I am still talking into earth's microphone
          willy nilly
    —to come back as words ghostly hued
          by early death
   but written so bodied
        mature in another decade.
Chatty prophet
      of yr own loves, personal
      memory feeling fellow
   Poet of building-glass
I see you walking you said with your tie
    flopped over your shoulder   in the wind down 5th Avenue
      under the handsome breasted workmen
        on their scaffolds ascending Time
          & washing the windows of Life
—off to a date with Martinis & a blond
      beloved poet far from home
        —with thee and Thy sacred Metropolis
   in the enormous bliss   of a long afternoon
   where death is the shadow
      cast by Rockerfeller Center,
          over your intimate street.

Who were you, black suited, hurrying to meet,
      Unsatisfied one?
                  Unmistakable,
                        Darling date
for the charming solitary/young poet with a big cock
                  who could fuck you all night long
                        till you never came,
      trying your torture on his/obliging fond body
      eager to satisfy god's whim that made you
                  Innocent, as you are.
I tried/your boys and found them ready
      sweet and amiable
            collected gentlemen
                  with large sofa apartments
lonesome to please   for pure language;
And you mixed with money
            because you knew enough language to be rich
                  If you wanted your walls to be empty—
Deep philosophical terms   dear Edwin Denby   serious as Herbert Read
with silvery hair   announcing   your dead gift
to the crowd   whose great op art   frisson
was the new sculpture your swollen blue wounded body made in the Universe
      when you went away   to Fire Island for the weekend
tipsy with a crowd of decade-olden friends

Peter stares out the window   at robbers
      distracted   in Amphetamine
and I stare into my head   & look for your/broken roman nose
      your wet mouth-smell of martinis
            & a big artistic tipsy kiss.
40's only half a life   to have filled
      with so many fine parties and evenings'
      interesting drinks together with one
                  faded friend or new
                  understanding social cat . . .
I want to be there in your garden party in the clouds
            all of us naked
strumming our harps and reading each other   new poetry
      in the boring celestial
            friendship Committee Museum.

You're in a bad mood?
                Take an Asprin.
                        In the Dumps?
                    I'm falling asleep
                            safe in your thoughtful arms.
Someone uncontrolled by History would have to own Heaven,
                                    on earth as it is.
I hope you satisfied your childhood love
        Your puberty fantasy   your sailor punishment on your knees
                            your mouth-suck
Elegant insistancy
                on the honking self-prophetic Personal
                as Curator of funny emotions to the mob,
Trembling one, whenever possible.   I see New York thru your eyes
        and hear of one funeral a year nowadays—
                        From Billie Holiday's time
                    appreciated more and more
a common ear
                        for our deep gossip.

                                            July 29 1966

HOLY GHOST ON THE NOD OVER THE BODY OF BLISS

Is this the God of Gods, the one I heard about
in memorized language universities murmer?
Dollar bills can buy it ! the great substance
exchanges itself freely through all the world's
poetry money, past & future currencies
issued & redeemed by the identical bank,
electric monopoly after monopoly owl-eyed
on every one of 90 million dollarbills vibrating
to the pyramid-top in the United States of Heaven—
Aye aye Sir Owl Oh say can you see in the dark you
observe Minerva nerveless in Nirvana because
Zeus rides reindeer thru Bethlehem's blue sky.
It's Buddha sits in Mary's body waving Kuan
Yin's white hand at the Yang-tze that Mao sees,
tongue of Kali licking Krishna's soft blue lips.
Chango holds Shiva's prick, Ouroboros eats th' cobalt bomb,
Parvati on YOD's perfumed knee cries Aum
& Santa Barbara rejoices in the alleyways of Brindaban
La Illaha El (lill) Allah Who   Allah Akbar!
Goliath struck down by kidneystone, Golgothas grow old,
all these wonders are crowded in Mind's Eye,
Superman & Batman race forward, Zarathustra on Coyote's ass,
Laotzu disappearing at the gate, God mocks God,
Job sits bewildered that Ramakrishna is Satan
and Bodhidharma forgot to bring Nothing.

December 1966

T.V. BABY POEMS

ALLEN GINSBERG

NEW YORK 1968

This book has been designed & printed by Cape Goliard
Press Ltd., London, for joint publication with Grossman
Publishers Inc., 125A East 19th Street, New York;
in an edition consisting of 1,750 soft cover & 750 case–
bound copies.

Illustrations by Allen Ginsberg & The Great Crystal.

Photograph by Malcolm Hart.

Printed in Great Britain